ASSEMBLING A GHOST

BY THE SAME AUTHOR

POETRY
The Collector and Other Poems
The Nature of Cold Weather and Other Poems
At the White Monument and Other Poems
The Force and Other Poems
Work in Progress
Dr Faust's Sea-Spiral Spirit and Other Poems
Three Pieces for Voices
The Hermaphrodite Album (with Penelope Shuttle)
Sons of My Skin: Selected Poems 1954–74
From Every Chink of the Ark
The Weddings at Nether Powers
The Apple-Broadcast and Other New Poems
The Working of Water
The Man Named East and Other New Poems
The Mudlark Poems & Grand Buveur
The Moon Disposes: Poems 1954–1987
In the Hall of the Saurians
The First Earthquake
Dressed as for a Tarot Pack
Under the Reservoir
The Laborators
My Father's Trapdoors
Abyssophone

FICTION
In the Country of the Skin
The Terrors of Dr Treviles (with Penelope Shuttle)
The Glass Cottage
The God of Glass
The Sleep of the Great Hypnotist
The Beekeepers
The Facilitators, or, Madam Hole-in-the-Day
The One Who Set Out to Study Fear
The Cyclopean Mistress

PLAYBOOKS
Miss Carstairs Dressed for Blooding and Other Plays
In the Country of the Skin

PSYCHOLOGY AND SPIRITUALITY
The Wise Wound (with Penelope Shuttle)
The Black Goddess and the Sixth Sense
Alchemy for Women (with Penelope Shuttle)

ASSEMBLING
A GHOST

Peter Redgrove

CAPE POETRY

First published 1996

1 3 5 7 9 10 8 6 4 2

© Peter Redgrove 1996

Peter Redgrove has asserted his right
under the Copyright, Designs and Patents Act 1988
to be identified as the author of this work

First published in the United Kingdom in 1996 by Jonathan Cape,
Random House, 20 Vauxhall Bridge Road, London SW1V 2SA

Random House Australia (Pty) Limited
20 Alfred Street, Milsons Point, Sydney,
New South Wales 2061, Australia

Random House New Zealand Limited
18 Poland Road, Glenfield,
Auckland 10, New Zealand

Random House South Africa (Pty) Limited
Box 2263, Rosebank 2121, South Africa

Random House UK Limited Reg. No. 954009

A CIP catalogue record for this book is available from the British Library

Papers used by Random House UK Limited are natural,
recyclable products made from wood grown in sustainable forests.
The manufacturing processes conform to the environmental
regulations of the country of origin.

ISBN 0–224–04482–6

Printed and bound in Great Britain
by Mackays of Chatham PLC

CONTENTS

ACKNOWLEDGEMENTS

Acknowledgements are due to the following:

Carolina Quarterly, Enitharmon, Manhattan Review, Orbis, Rialto, Terrible Work, The Times Literary Supplement, Verse

ESHER

The two suns,
The sun in the sea, the sun in the sky:
The bicycle of summer.

Do I deserve it,
Shirt open to my breastbone as I ride?

My shirt billowing like more lungs,
Like sunny clouds
On my summer bicycle,

The dawn wind
Smelling like a scrubbed deck.

Later, the sky of an uncolour –
Pale as a grey cat's fur,
Or ancient glassware
Rubbed misty in the desert.
Do I deserve it?

The garden birds flow up out of the lilac,
The gulls
Hang up by one wing and wheel around.

The bicyclist with all Esher
In his shirt, kept
Warm and sunny there.

BIBLIOPHILE

Because of Falmouth
He has more Bibles than he has shirts.
He will search out Jerusalem with candles.

Falmouth seems undersea,
Or it brims with the understructure of the clouds,
With invisibly salted water and mist

Which webs everything into one great mansion,
A mansion turning all the time,
An invisible manor-house greater than any human home.

Staircases, dungeons, great slam-gates,
Sequent chambers, draughty galleries, speed past me,
Secret passages disclosed, lifts on their hawsers,

On their salt ropes ascending
Momentary high towers whose shafts
Exclaim with sunshine and open to the foundations.

What does the Bible give to an unbeliever?
The Bible has fullness.
Fullness stops the mind being wiped

By Falmouth, that is my prayer
As I shut my shirt to my chin and open my Bible
Every time the clouds

Blow in from the East, on that East wind
Which has holes opening in it, bible-deep.

KISSING THIRST AWAY

The condoms in their illustrated wrappings.
The old long man who puts on a new suit each day.

A smooth lake in the picture above the bed
With the solitary figure of a horse bending to drink:

Its velvet lips from that first touch or water-kiss
Pluck the entire water into a concentric ripple-system

Which searches into all the eminent hillsides
And sudden fastnesses.

Thus it is, in their bed; this is why
The picture was chosen to hang there

(To kiss the place and to see above a lake
Something like a light generated in the air,

Or, the seagull pirouettes on just such a spot
Situated in the tail of his roof-consort –

He pirouettes, the wings suspending him
Just on the point of his feathery entered penis

Which kisses the whole lake, his horse
Kisses their thirst away).

PORTALS

I

The water darkens before
The grey clouds, light
At the bottom of the garden
Is bent double, folded
Like a lens magnifying
Ships on the lake;

Cloud-shadow strides
Down over the yellow hill-fields
With rapid, concise, large
Movements. The lake's edge
Intervenes and the vast shadows become
Evenly spread in its roughened surface,

And darken there, in deeper shadows,
Even before the sky truly darkens.

II

They are like Arabian carpets
Travelling under a spell

Both above the ocean
And within it,

Fleets of speedy
Arabian medusae. Despite
All this darkness
Arranging itself
Piecemeal in lake and sky

4

The sun is a mirror on fire
Hollowing out shapes with its shadows,

With slant shadows of the rocks
Creating every kind of doorway,
Portal, threshold, boundary, slant lintel
And domain.

THE ROCKPOOL FLY

The fossil bones of great saurians
Brought out of the clay
During the building. The castle
Stands floodlit
On its mass of dolomite
Like the rocks' further thoughts
About rock – look!
I am hollow, I have
Inhabitants, my stones
Are not sealed,
I can spire.

Moreover in the castle's
Laboratories its mistress
Breeds by genetic engineering
A rockpool fly

That in its growth
From egg to imago
Takes up the gold in the seawater
And shucks at every ecdysis
This golden image

So the rock pools at the castle's foot
Fill with hollow statues
Of this fly in gold.

'Which is greater,
The beauty or the profit?'
Asks the rock of the castle;
'The pleasure of my mistress
As she furnishes these rooms
With the profit of beauty,'

Replies the castle
Full with the images
And the light from the images.

OPEN SECRETS CHATEAU

I

The chateau chambers
Simulate a forest and the forest
Resembles chateaux; their lords
Walk and whistle through the upper storeys,
And light pours in their verdant casement windows,
And paces down the stairs, carrying candles.

II

With the heirs I walk
Through this great-bodied house
Or among the trees which move like visionaries
Of when they will become chateau panels
And secret doors in galleries
Which slide aside as the wind speaks,
And slide to; the wind says something else.

III

I turn a corner, find a fresh staircase
Of unanticipated skylights where sun pours in;
The slightest breeze shifts these cloudscapes
Though each cloud weighs
Heavily as a forest, heavily
As granite chateaux which lightly walk
Sires of light out of their sunframed pictures.

ST STAINES' NIGHT

I

The quietest moment of the night
Transferred to glass;
Somebody shining a mirror at me
From the far side of the valley.

II

The woman's bridal scowl, her thick plait
A tawny coil, to which as she came in
She whispered urgently, over her shoulder.

III

The woman's bridal scowl peeling
The mirrors off the walls, then
Rehanging them, multiplied.

IV

That momentary leaping flame from
The other side of the valley, flashes
Like taking a snap with a camera full of sun.

V

He unwinds her plait greedily, taking pleasure
From each fisted tug on her
Colossal braid; all her power
Was in her hair, he undid her somehow
And shook it out and she

Was another woman. A sky
Smocked with stars. The hoop of her sex.

VI

It was St Staines' Night and a breath of moon
Went through the house, dust in all its shapes
Rose and followed.

KILLING THE RUST

The flies snapped in the blast
Like nodules of perfume.

The street theatre, nay, opera;
And the open-air theatre
Of the deck of the ship
In dry dock; the theatrical
Arc light thrusting stiff shadows
Vibrating as the steel does
To its riveters and their percussion,

The big bells uttering
Through the soles of the feet, the hulls,
The shucks of the ships

Then men like clowns
Clad in big suits
Of dayglo colour
And they are in charge
Of orange fire
And violet electricity

Like daffodils in their hardhats
The acrobats on their platforms
The chasms into the ships opened wide
As by ladder into the sea
And the white horses should come
Puffing up the flights of ladders
But it throngs and buckles there
With the violet light and ripped shadows
Of the arc's glare repairing the arks

And the plumes without saddle
Lift far out in the bay

The man who kills the red rust
The man hanging on his trapeze
With his paint-gun sealing the rust
Closing the red books
That open without cease everywhere

It darkens like a night-vessel

Scaffold creating scaffold
The big openwork cranes
Like wheeling trapeze
Nipping up the small performers
Tiny acrobats in their immense hooks
Like Spanish queries.

DAVY JONES' LIONESS

There was a siege of dreams
Of needing or wanting
To buy a new watch; almost
It slipped away as I paused
By the Xmas display of actual watches, spoke

To the woman serving in dark suit
And pearls, of the beauty
Of the pearl display on dark velvet
(Meaning herself also)

We agreed they were pretty
And what a pity it was
That men did not wear them. I informed her
I had gone out in the heavy male
Serpentine beads and they interested the women
Just as they liked my sporting
A pigtail, and she said

She could see that, and why had I
Not put them on to visit her? this was unspoken,
And now she paced
Like a small dark lioness,
Her movement round the shop
Had been increasing, I could not
Keep track and she seemed
As she moved to roar subsonically
Through the open maw of her black suit
While I told her that a stranger
In the pub had kissed me because

I wore beads and she did not know

That men could, and I said yes,
As you see, they can; but,

Said the dark lioness, does that
Include pearls? she was pacing now
Up and down the jeweller's stairs while I
Looked again at the watches, remembering my dream
Of needing a watch and she watched me
Because it was a dream in which
I had remembered my dream, and this was why
She came and roared at me
Soundlessly in her dark. The bijouterie
With its beauties shedding
Their light everywhere was now charged
With the subsonic breath of pearls;

It was like lions in an aviary,
It was the singular oyster-shop of pearls,
Of pearls and glittering innuendo;
The slime of the sea necklaced round
The long neck of the dark assistant,
The cabinets full of ticking salt
Sea-jewels telling me the tide was rising;
This was Davy Jones' Locker
Full of ivory-treasures, tides and gems,
That is the watch of watches, and she?
Davy Jones' Lioness from the Orient
Now wearing pearls that gathered
Like rain under the sea.

ENÝPNION

A bee in the library
Of elm books and oak books,
Holly shelves,
Ivy shelves,
The drowsy-house,
The dreamlike slumber in books;

Polishing the windows
Of the drowsy-house
That open to and fro
One sees out of the leaves;

I open the book and its honey runs over,
The supple binding polished with beeswax,
The dark-veined pages,
The whispering leaves
Inscribed with sentences that hum
In the amber twilight,

A gentleman's library
In which to drowse
That is full of Virgil
Who has retired,
Who has finished with all
Heroes larger than beesize.

IRON AGE

As they worked the meteorite with silex hammers,
'Your knives – where are they obtained?'
Asked Cortez of the Aztec chiefs,
Who simply pointed upwards, to the sky.

Meteoric iron was the valuta, superseding gold,
Aeroliths weighted with stellar sanctity skidding to earth,
Ore speeding from elsewhere, trophy of the beyond;

And the one who makes a sword,
Beating the iron fallen from heaven into stars,
Is naturally invulnerable as those stars; and this Smith
Strikes his anvil so that nature feels

Through all her pores the enormous revelry.

THE SPOOR

He enjoyed feeling the warmth
Of girls' bottoms
Spread on the train seats
They had just vacated.
If it were possible to do so
Unobserved, he would bend swiftly
And smell their smell. He called this
'Sniffing the bouquet of the Sphinx.'

He held also that the traces
Which great music leaves on
The air are a beneficent ozone,
And loves to sniff wild flowers
In a buttonhole
To music.

He still has not smelt
The bouquet of the woman with bruised arms
Who now wakes
And tries to retune the shattered radio
Out of its stuttering static.
She inspects her arms
And imagines they are bruised
Only with the marks her dreams
Make on her.

She has ten blouses –
Why choose the white one starched
Stiff as a sail,
Its tucks waxy with starch,
Its whiteness like the white comber
Or a herself-wave gone

Queenly-still and
Articulated like a crustacean?

She is guarding
Against his love, making
Herself look like an
Odourless assemblage and a
Figure carved out of white noise
Like a dentist's coat
In the shriek of his drill.

But this is how he discovered
The spoor, and tracked
To her snowy heart, where
He found his own bouquet stirring,
His own identity-smell, crest of the wave,
And proffered it; the blouse
Opened of its own accord, and the air
Opened between them.

THE GHOST FROM CHESSINGTON

The clear-running tide
Bites at his feet, he
Dances out of the way
Of the razor-cool wavelets packed
With the Rapier-Fish; he identifies too
The Father-Lasher, or Sting-Fish
Ready for affray, he escapes

Into the wood, for its dry beauties.

Here is the Death's Head Hawk
On whose bark he admires
The profound Zen-sketches
Of the human face-bone
Done with a bushy brush;
Night-familiars which are
Accordingly his kin, boneface,
The night-side of butterflies. This moth
Can squeak or squeal, and is fond
Of honey; a naked skull
Drinking at a bowl of honey. He lays out
Also sugar-lumps for the flying skulls.

He notes the Bohemian Waxwings
Feeding in a berry-laden Mountain
Ash tree (no need to cater here) and looks out
For the Small Elephant Hawk whose time it is
At dusk to feed upon the blooms
Of Campion, Stock, Valerian and Sweet William;

Here they are
In the dim light at their pulsing feast
Of the flowers wrapped in night-odours.

Well and good, I have seen to my charge.
Now it is time to drink my own
Favoured nectars at the all-night tavern,

Where I may sustain such bruises
As will shorten my days
From shots of alcohol, and unleaf,
As I sip, the pictures of my skull

To flutter through the woods and feed
On the honey I have left
And spread out for them.

LEATHER GOODS

I feel emptied by the thunderstorm. She
Looks as I feel. He takes me behind the shop
To show me the source of the leather with which
He makes his wonderful supple skirts, waistcoats,
Tabards, luggage, including doctors' bags. I must
Conceal the origin, he says, handing me her skin
Perfectly tanned, hanging it over my arm, it is heavy
As the ulster of a big man, the hands bear nails
Which are as fresh as any person's living,
I cannot see the expression, her hair
Brushes the planking. He tells me

It was a pleasure-steamer wrecked
Off the Manacles and the bones
Gently rolled out of them and their leather
Brine-tanned in a volcanic undersea stream
That was sulphurous;

'The diver into that wardrobe,
She came in one evening, when I was closing,
With a beautifully supple Gladstone bag, out of it pulled
A total body-suit with nails complete and a zip
"I can deliver five hundred," she said;
"The leather breathes, but is warm still
In sub-arctic chills," "There's
Little call for this degree
Of warm clothing here," I said,

' "Then shut your eyes," she said. I felt
A little soft cool hand steal
Into my own, it was comforting. "Let me take
Just the hands, six dozen at first, see how they go . . ."

'Under the sea the teeth rolled
Away like pearls as the gums rotted, scoured
Into white sand. The hair
Continued growing all those years, hiding the wreck
Like a head of hair itself, with full tidal tresses;
Out of that undulant harvest the diver plucked her
    fortune.'

SENSORIA

I

Dew-soaked spiders' webs give their owners
Essential drinking-water, the whole waterworks
Laid out in its glossy coiling pipes
And its straight pipes, like the radials
Of a city with at its suburbs
The spider kneeling
Ready to sip it all up — the sparking round firework.

The waterworks floats
Like a gossamer crowded with beads,
In every bead you can see all the others,
Celestial waterworks

Eaten and rebuilt each day, for the lungs
Need frequent watering, the thirsty eater
The garden-cross spider, the crossing
Shewing across her back,
Yet she is thirsty again and must lay out
Her plans of piping and adhesive —

Eating the web
Improves the quality of the glue,
Essence of the insect-trap —
(Dancing out on the city-straight lines,
Gobbling up the beads,
Gobbling the thoroughfare of headlights).

II

Trenches slotted
In the sand-dunes where the wind

Has dug them out; in the evening
They brim with dry warm air
Pleasant to step into and wade across.

This air is flavoured by the grass,
Its quality or bouquet, and its warmth,
Its movement, which cohere
In a ghost-paw face-pat.

May God polish your books!
The sands are bound with
Juniperus Cozii which is
Himalayan Juniper;
Because of its immortal quality
The Chinese recommend it
For coffins,
Perfumed coffins.

From ASSEMBLING A GHOST

MS POTTER

A smile painted red
Signifying mastery of oral sex,
Teeth white as the Moon,
And an amazed 'Oh!'
From the warm blackness –
Having shown that chord of colours:
Red, white and the deep
Black of her spoken merriment;

Now she sits down at her wheel
In her death-clothes
Creating the algorithm
Of the Potter who made us all
With her belly-art, and winks
And throws down clay
With a slap on her spinning
Wheel, and she catches it
With her fingers as it
Shoots away in loops –
And immediately form rears up,
A low vase of hers spins in
Pulses from shallow to deep
And back again, storing darkness
In the bowl of the vase, then
Dismissing it, thumb-forcing
The shadow out of the bowl in
This messy cave with
Its mud-splashes, puddles,
A hissing tap. Her smock
Is filthy-stiff. There is a streak
Of clay across her cheek while

The zinc perfume of the stinging earth
And high velocity mud shoots
Off the wheel-rim, this makes the place
So real that almost every gesture now
Hypnotised by the wheel falls
Into the ritual,
The vase deepening
Like the night-sky forming
In the potter's thighs
Her fingers digging
In the spinning void
That falls exactly
Into the tall vase-walls:
Central night, with stars of wet clay;

I needed to spin my heirs
On her wheel
Like a meteor-swarm, the children
Pushing and shoving to get in
The stout thumb and the gracile fingers
Opening the door in her death-clothes

A door is opened
To the yard and birds
With the cool faces of virgins
Pace over the threshold, pick their crumbs
From the bread-rolls tall as vases.

I sit patiently on the uncomfortable
Stool made of a late-mediaeval
Crosshead; the heiroglyphs are swarming
Again as she peddles at the wheel, the hypnotic vase
Pulsing with shadow, then shallowing
To a vibrant bowl; she is interested
In the brown and carrot-shaped

Amphoras made of Nile mud; this is how
The wines of Egypt were transported;

She, by chucking and spinning
Has constructed just such a bottle; I cannot help it —
I picture her at her wheel of light and shadow;
It needs to be oblivion wine from such a bottle.

SUPERSTITION

Has buried in the pleasance a coil
Of the newest and the brightest vintage,
Places fruit and wine on the cold hearth-log,
A bread-loaf on the step in the well.

All done, the house made safer for it,
She comes, as butter comes in the churn,
Gripping the paddle.

Walking, the all-night carnival
Flares on the turfy wasteland beach, the full moon
A silver wheel that dips into the sea,
The Ferris Wheel snapping with stars like fireworks,
The Fairies' Wheel, its orbits ridden
By whom? I take up the glasses to see,
I am gripped, as

Mud is bewitched by grass, grass by cattle,
Cattle by maidens milking; white comes out of the dark,
Gold out of the white; as butter
Comes in the churn, dawn grips.

LITTERY-BUGGERY

Z observes that there are
No colour-clashes in nature, she gazing
At green on green, red berries
And white blossom on green hawthorn;

But the clashes on the picnic meadow
Are audible three fields away.

It is the picnickers with their percussion shell-suits
In orange and mauve, magenta and voltage blue,
Their yellow yellower than a thousand suns –

For the great German chemists
Devised new anilines to cause
A shriek to be generated against Nature
Without turning on a single transistor;

Out of the horse-collar hollows stick
Faces, baggy, creased, bloat screwed up
Against the self-noise –

The intention was to ghetto this littery-buggery
Away in the Midland cities once and for all,
But they have come out again in their shells over the
     water-meadows,

Bringing out their sheer suits that need
To be vivid enough to state something about the city air;

Look, they are struggling out of their
Headlight-colours, their neon statements;
Do not throw these shells away, I fear you will need them
     again,

These nursery paintings worn to keep the buzz in
Whatever auroras of soot sift from the tall chimneys:

We shall need this technological suiting
To keep the pollution on the outside, all of us:

This man wears his angry orange on the outside
To denote his great peace within.

SOME ELIXIR

I

I am releasing like music
A great spirit of new-mown grass,
A spirit of happiness composed
Of sticky grass-hormone
And music from the house,
I am mowing grass under the apple-trees,
The windfalls explode in my warbling blades,
The pigs scuttle away from my whooping engines.

II

The shrubbery is thick with
Creeper and prickbush
As detailed as the music.

An orange fly
Hovers in front of my face
Gazing full into my eyes
With its gold eighteenth-century spectacles.

The hogs in the orchard munch to the music,

The child skips and runs, toys with her shadow
Or the shadow of a bird, to music.

Humans photosynthesise;
When the sun goes in, happiness
And sugar-production come to a standstill.

III

Pigs crisp-munch the windfalls;
Rooting under the orchard-canopies,
They belly-swell with ferment of cider and applesauce,

Apple-flavouring their pork alas.

My mower catarrhs on a windfall, resumes its reaping.

IV

Here comes the sun again, with the music.
Music pours from the wholeskin windows
Of the great electrostatic castles buoyant above,
A broad road of perfume unrolls down here
Over the rose-garden walls, the invisible red carpet
To the heavenly doors
Of heavy gold pollen in the flower's centre.

V

Mowing the grass, slicing open by the neck
All the slender dream-bottles of happiness-hormone,
All the endorphin-vintages laid down by the grass;
Is it long panels of visible fresh-cut
Grass-smell I see plating the meadows,
Or long roads cast by the sinking sun?
Who puts the sun out before I have finished,
Who rolls up the red carpet to the rose's centre?
A grey ghost of autumn seizes me at sunset,
I make no more sugar, or happiness hormone.
I have finished the lawn and the orchard.
I will look for my wife in the house
And see if she has saved some elixir for us.

TO CIRCE

I

I was that hero again
Struggling up

Out of my time as hog,
Astonished at my upright carriage,

The rolling boulder of my skull,
My complicated hands,

The shake of my knees,
The savagery of my thoughts:

I wept and cursed – I was a man again.

II

Pieces of that piggery-paradise came with me,
The white clouds persisted

In the dazzling pools of filth;
The pine-forest retained pig-heat,

The shock of tallness
In the serious balsam of the pointing avenues,

The thunder unfolding
Like the black diamond of the Sorceress,

That is, the woman wearing her lucky raincoat
In the lucky rain,

Out and feeding the pigs their magical slop,
Shining, as they shone.

NUDE STUDIES VI: THE HORSE

She is in love with the canoe-faces of horses,
Their violin smile. Riding them
Naked skin to skin

Is to sail close to the symphonic brink of the known
    world.
It amazes her that entering the pub
Of kisses, basket meals, stout decals, accelerando

Chatter, is to plunge
Into a rubbish-tip of bright plastic and broken
Radio-sets still working though they

Have been thrown away; yet after a beer or two
It is eating one's Good Food inside a Christmas Tree;
And this marvel is nothing

To the sonorous breathing of the horse
She rode yesterday skin to skin
Up to the vast water-note

Of the reservoir from which the horse
As from a harp plucked water; the ripples
Of his drink reached out easily to the far shore.

FALMOUTH IN THE ASTRAL

I

When a high-octane thundercloud
Rushes in, shouting, the whole town
Of streets of houses shoots up like
Fields of wheat ripening fast-forward
To its sultry magnet; but only a few
Fully-ripened rocket ghosthouses
Loosen their foundations and fly away
Stripped of the bricks and mortar
Which stolidly remains and immediately starts to grow
A new astral, which may take twenty years.

The glittering spirit-houses
Which have escaped in flocks from cities
By shot-silk wings of electricity calmly
Settle in the white high tree-tops of the clouds.
Angel-houses, echoing.

II

Certain houses have mislaid their ghostly angels,
You cannot tell, when sitting in one room, where
The other people sit, the walls are quite opaque.
In these lost houses even the owners
Get lost. But other houses crack like chrysalids
And out of the shell the inner houses clamber
And raise themselves like blossoming heavens
Or Hampton Courts fitted to miles of Hampton Courts.
My kitchen becomes a regal porte-cochère; in bed
I lie on the ocean-floor, in the wine-cellarage; such homes
Are opulent, millionairish, whatever your circumstances
You never get lost in these houses, you

Have the knowledge of them, they are
The architecture that extends far beyond
The appearance of things.

III

The doorchimes pling-plong twice, I open
The front door on the fresh electrical air,
There is no one there; it is the former owner
Arriving home, and when the chimes sound
A door opens in the door through which
He passes where he is more truly indoors
Than he has ever been before. I lift
The daffodils in the vase and let them drop
So they arrange themselves, I look
Into their wells or throats full of light
Where pollen processes through the cells
I must call mansions; they are full of light:
Lamps which are mansions held up
By the flower which is a city.

BOY'S PORRIDGE

I

She serves me my round plate of porridge
Pocked with craters. It is the Full Moon
I am eating, smiling up at Mum. 'Where
Does porridge come from?' 'Down the chimney, son.'

'Why *morning* porridge?' 'It is the Moon.
We don't eat it at night. It is out of reach.'
The Moon like Santa Claus
Delivering sacks of cold porridge down the chimney.

II

My next-day's breakfast plate riding high,
Brightening the clouds. Mother pins
Her moonstone to her collar to serve me
My boy's porridge; like a full moon rising
Through maternal skies, it rides her breath.

There is cinder-snapping as the hearth-fire cools;
I go out into the night to watch the scudding
Ashes in the sky, and the round clinker riding
That burns with a cold fire. As I return

Hungry for porridge the sun rises over the sea:
Fleets of jellyfish bump in the tide
Like salty bubbles in moon-porridge
Set to boil on the hob.

EXISTING

The balsams of the heath
Roll out of the stone and from the ling also;
The boulders brim where they are
With heat and perfume, each like a person.

There was something about my nap,
A kind of hypnotism,
For I and the world were one.

I was woken from it by the gulls
Whose cries sounded in my half-sleep
Like babies soothed by wooden pipes,

So I walked out in the evening air
Among the day-warm stones set like tables,

Cartographers' tables,
With landmass lichen-scrolls tacked to the stone;
And the heath swarmed with psyches or moths
Who settled over the warm stones
Their feathery bosoms and cigar-plump bellies
And spread their chart-wings of constellations
Over the lichen-maps' earthy projections.

SALE

The fever had passed.
She felt cool and dry.
She asked: 'Why
Don't we take a drive
Over the hills?' It was perhaps
Too soon after the fire.
Mother was ironing palls,
And the lake was shaking the hills.

There had been a cellar-fire
Breaking through the racks
Of dust-and-spiderweb-silted
Bottles,

Caused by the old liqueurs
Starting to work again,
For the flame was wildfire
Like brandy-flame
Blue as electricity
That does not scorch the hand;

The fire was harmless and amazing,
Like the round flame of a Christmas pudding,
Clasping the church roof,
Flapping over it like a pall.

The sparks from a shattered bottle
Igniting the webs – spider-fire?

Were the firemen still hosing?
There was nothing to hose, no.
They have disappeared into the rectory

Leaving behind that aura
Which hangs around shut-down machinery.

Mother said: 'Your sons
Could help on the farm,
Your daughters in the house,
Filling the place
With friendly faces.'

Daddy lifted her up
And swung her round again.
The bright lake
Blinded her when he did that,
The lake that carried over its surface
Like a loudspeaker made of water
The dislocated sounds of trucks
Rumbling out over the overpass.

It was a dissonance
Which changed the look of the water
That magnified it. A winter look
Now of cold fragments where peak
Would not connect with lake,
Lake would not reflect peak
And shivered it,
Gave it the water's trembling
That solid rock
Blurred by the matt waves. As these lorries
Passed through the town the shopwindows
Cursed at them in French: SALE SALE SALE.

WHEAL CUPID

Thunder over lake, a beating
Of wings over the skin
Of the lake, two blue dragonflies
With thunder in their wings
Thunder; whose shaking
Is in the lake.

Two sky-skinned dragonflies
Bent like twin tempered blades
Shuddering, sip
From each other;

Tempered dragonflies reined
Into a smooth loop, thunder
Negotiated with wings
Darting, then stone-still;
Hoop spins over the lake;

The feet of the dragons
Running through thunder

Their lightning plashes everywhere.

THE VIRGIN OF FALMOUTH

*'Wherefore art thou red in thin apparel, and thy garments
like him that treadeth in the wine-vat?'*

She was taken by car to hear the midnight mass.
On the way the rain in the moonlight
Rose over the hills
Like a gigantic man on a bone-white horse.

The church organ was like an aeroplane engine broken
    open
So that its cylinders should provide
Only soft and slow explosions.

She was told that her skin and clothes
Were tuned to several realities,
Was shown how to angle and open her cape and hood
To mingle the odorous souls of body with head;
Was given a hard Laxton, and told to bite into it;
The juices streamed.

It was the flexible curcubite of her dress
And the stars embroidered on it
Directed these distillations,
So, when she opened it, heaven opened;

Then when each person came up to the altar on which
    she sat,
To kiss her,
The frank incense of her apple-breath
Parted like a wedding-veil.

And she read the title gold-lettered
The Bodiless One, on the black lectern-book;

'How can that be!' she cried, understanding at once,
And she took the great book in her arms;
The tall chapters of print
Were columns of perfume, walking and waking with her;

Then the people in the church pulled the tall doors open –
She shed her starry robe and dropped her book –
The smell of dawn rode into the church
Like the perfume of the rain-lord riding in:

A bodiless high-mounted senior on a sunbeam horse.

BETTER THAN BEFORE

Hard as I tried
I could not
Turn into a pig.
My companions duly changed,
This meant they were set free.

I had no thought of rescuing
Anybody, or ever returning
To my wife and son — no,
I had travelled to this island
With my seafaring friends
To beg our freedom from Circe
By being turned into pigs.

We each of us paid our fee
In transformation-gold,
And my successful friends
Dropped to their little hooves
And began grunting, and worrying
With their leathery noses and telescope nostrils
Into the ground which had to them
Become a nutrient god. Some scuttled
Into the forest-fringes for truffles,
Others wallowed in a compost
Of auto-urine, rolling
Over and over in the spiritual mud.

I dropped on my knees
To Circe and I could see that she
By making faces wrestled with her magic,
But no joy — I was a man still. I
Threw myself into the mud and rolled
Where my companions had rolled, but

It was no go. Circe came too
Attire and all, turned into mud,
Hoping to distract me with piggishness
But I ran on into the sea
To wash the slimy stench away, and Circe
Followed, her clothes and self
Turned into the very waves, into membraneous jewels
In the salt sunshine slippery like exterior cunt,
Dressed in the whole sea – success! for
This epiphany drew me from thoughts
Of my privileged companions, and
Copulating in the foam, I forgot them all
In this other privilege. In due course

Circe withdrew their freedom
From my friends as the gold ran out,
And they stood up, better than before.
The ship's carpenter, that good-for-nothing,
Was now a master of his craft, as we found
When he rebuilt our ship from the
Storm-shattered fragments. The Master-at-Arms
Was now a dancer, whose dance
Was the perfection of his martial arts.
Cook stood up a gourmet able to sustain
And interest the hero-stomachs through
The long voyages, hunting or cultivating
All the food he cooked. As for myself,
Still myself, how could I
Further our quest? What was I for?

It was obvious – after the years
With Circe I had become
The ship's lover of women, assured passport,
The glittering one, riding into the harbours

Like the tide itself, salt-prow
Qualified king-person to each fresh landfall.

ABBATOIR BRIDE

Slow-working in the slaughterhouse
On a showery day. He holds out
A bloody fillet in his icy hands.
I pop with sweat. Bleed out, sparkle!

There are flies like lacquered idols, skulls
The size of sand-grains humming like nuns,
Exquisite religious sculpture vibrating
To the note of that god-gong, the sun,
Flies carved again as with knives, risen
Out of the food-chest with ivory clasps,
Shut into the meat, it seems, by him let out
With his shining knives and his shadow of flies,
His marriage-property, sturdy and obscene.

And there is a leaf-marriage too, the sun lying
In panels and yellow shadows on the path,
The flies in intermediary shady swarms
Celebrating the marriage of meat and sun;

And this little rain marries all the leaves;
The sealed chamber, this vagina
Is like a bird flying
Through the rain, drenched,
Beak wide as a fledgling straining for the worm;

He has opened many creatures, this one
Opens itself, alive, without violation,
However loud the sun, with its darkening flies.

AROMATHERAPY

I

Loose clouds blow with their shadows, drop silence
Into this fold of the hills, so that kissing
Among the silence trees is like plunging
Lips into a bed of wild flowers;

Geranium, the intimate; *Narcissus*, the earthly hypnotist;
Cardomom, cleanser of the senses; *Star Jasmine*, mistressing
  the night.

II

Since a lofty spirit accumulates in underground caverns,
And because the ancient stones were redesigned
As permanent governing residences for the fluctuating
Spirits of the waters, accordingly
There is a hungry pressure up the ancient wellshaft
Of the Waterhouse Restaurant where two waters meet.

The diners do not know why they are famished.
'Well,' she says, 'well . . .' all her waters flowing,
Underground some weir is opening – 'Weird,' she remarks,
'Weird,' noticing with what emphasis
The blood of the rare steak stretches
Her nostrils and crimsons her creamed potatoes.

III

Neroli, the acutely female; *Jonquil*, exposer of heart's desires;
Rosemary, the gallant; *Lavender*, the steadier;
For the earth contains its own planets
Whose rays pierce its crust as flowers;
Standing in their thin vase on the dazzling table
Lamps that shed from below invisible starlight.

THEY COME

They come flickering down the lane
In their black-white,
White-black shirts and skirts
As the moon changes
White to black and back again,
White shirts, black waistcoats,
A lick of white petticoat
At the hem of a black skirt
Flickering down the lane,
The human flowers
Are black-white, white-black.

On the body, like amazement gathering,
The matters that arrive of themselves:
Hair breaks on chest, balls drop,
Voices break heartbreakingly, hips
Gather and round their pillars, and on the smooth chest
Tiny magnolias bud.

The homes turbulent
With strange new body-perfumes,
The black-and-white courtship moon-engine
Comes flickering down the lane.
How many of them meet there?
All? Or none? the white moonlight
Flickering through the branches.

'Development,' they say, as when you hold
A polaroid and watch the picture, the person
Stepping into the white space, like
The person you know stepping off the train
On to the platform; you saw him before
In his grandfather, his aunt.

The bones, white as photography
Hold the image of him for a certain time;
It fades off them to appear
Elsewhere, like a spirit, clothing itself
In black-white, white-black for the meeting in the lane.

ARROWHEADS

I

We shift the pile of arrowheads
Like leaves fallen from
A stone tree. We use raucous
Shovels and squeaky wheelbarrows
With wooden wheels sliced
From trees. It was a great
Workshop here in which the
Arrows for many deaths
Were fabricated by industrious
Ancient workers; I pocket one
In case it has my name on it, and
By so doing I can make myself
Safe in battle. Indeed, they
Will be sold as charms
In Tintagel, Glastonbury;
A well-made arrow sings
As it flies to the heart
And takes it
As a humming-bird the bloom.

II

The dead roosting in the treetops
At the site of their arrow-factory,
They crane out of the boughs to see
If we will use their products for
Their designed purpose – murder;

But we are shovelling them
Into our rustic wheelbarrows
For they are a fortune of charms

And we will sell them to all
The souvenir shops of Cornwall
(Black arrowheads, chipped
From an obsidian flint).

Round the great tree
Which sheltered these fletchers
As they worked twined the ancient serpent
Of the beginnings who was still
In paradise, breathing the balsams
Of its parks. The trees around us
Are in paradise still, even
The cruel arrowmakers are in paradise
Having finished their work and gone home
To roost in the wonderful trees; once
They liked to live in promontory forts
And kept for escape their large
Shallow-draught boats close to hand.

MOTH AND MOTORCAR

Moths rolling over and over
In the car lights,
The beams and rafters of light
Their widening rooms
Wedged open. The goldstone
Of the moths' eyes flashing.

We stood under a gigantic hedgerow,
Moths lying on the sheet
Like broken yachts.
Her breath took frosty forms
Like moths. She released
A potion from her cunt
As a moth might ooze its balsam
And fan it with its wings,
Her dress started this,
The night moths wished to gather
On its flowers. I was penetrated

By this balsam of hers
And by the balsam of the moths sticking
To the white sheet with their
Excited juice, I could not tell
Moth from lover, it was all natural.

We had laid the old double sheet
Down on the grass
In front of the blazing headlights,

We had laid it down
Like a gigantic marriage-ghost,
We smoothed out the creases
With their shadows, and fastened

The edges down with white stones.
The rest, it happened of itself,
Each moth a small lamp burning sperm-oil.

As the sheet darkened
With its night-progeny
Seeking to create a dress like hers,
Lying down, a night-dress statement,
The sheet an imaging mirror,

A linen mirror like a bridebed,
Moth neckline, moth-buttons,
Moths patterning a great moth,
We felt our skins darkening
Not just with what we saw but what was
Seen through the lighted
Balsams, human and non-human.

TRAVELLING LIBRARY

The Iceberg Street
That leads across the Atlantic,
A west wind on the Iceberg Way:
Those books were marble,
Chilled you as you tried
To turn the pages.

Those books were smoke –
They opened and blew away
Leaving a certain tang in the air.

This is an ideal book, warm
From the last reader,
Smelling of new-baked bread
As I split its crust;

Is very nourishing
And contains as well
A certain sleep,
A certain reader's resin
Which is the rhythm of the tale
That arises to the nose
As the pages warm,

And is its bonding,
Like a cat on the lap
Sends into your belly a fire;
Now, is your friend
Whether you like it or not;
The fey body of the book,
The brightness of its tiger-heart
Which is neither
Paper or ink.